j641.343 67351
Watts, Franklin.
Oranges /

NANUET PUBLIC LIBRARY
NANUET, NEW YORK

ORANGES

BY FRANKLIN WATTS

ILLUSTRATIONS BY ROBERT ULM

CHILDRENS PRESS, CHICAGO

Library of Congress Cataloging in Publication Data

Watts, Franklin.
　　Oranges.

　　SUMMARY: Discusses different types of oranges, where and how they are grown, and their uses.
　　1. Oranges—Juvenile literature. [1. Orange]
I. Ulm, Robert. II. Title.
SB370.07W38　　641.3′4′31　　77-16045
ISBN 0-516-03688-2

Copyright © 1978 by Regensteiner Publishing Enterprises, Inc.
All rights reserved. Published simultaneously in Canada.
Printed in the United States of America.

1 2 3 4 5 6 7 8 9 10 11 12 R 85 84 83 82 81 80 79 78

That juicy orange you sometimes eat is called a citrus fruit. It belongs to a group, or genus, known as *citrus.* Grapefruit, lemons, and limes are citrus fruits, too.

There are many kinds of oranges, perhaps more than a hundred different types. But the kind you see and eat most often is the "sweet orange."

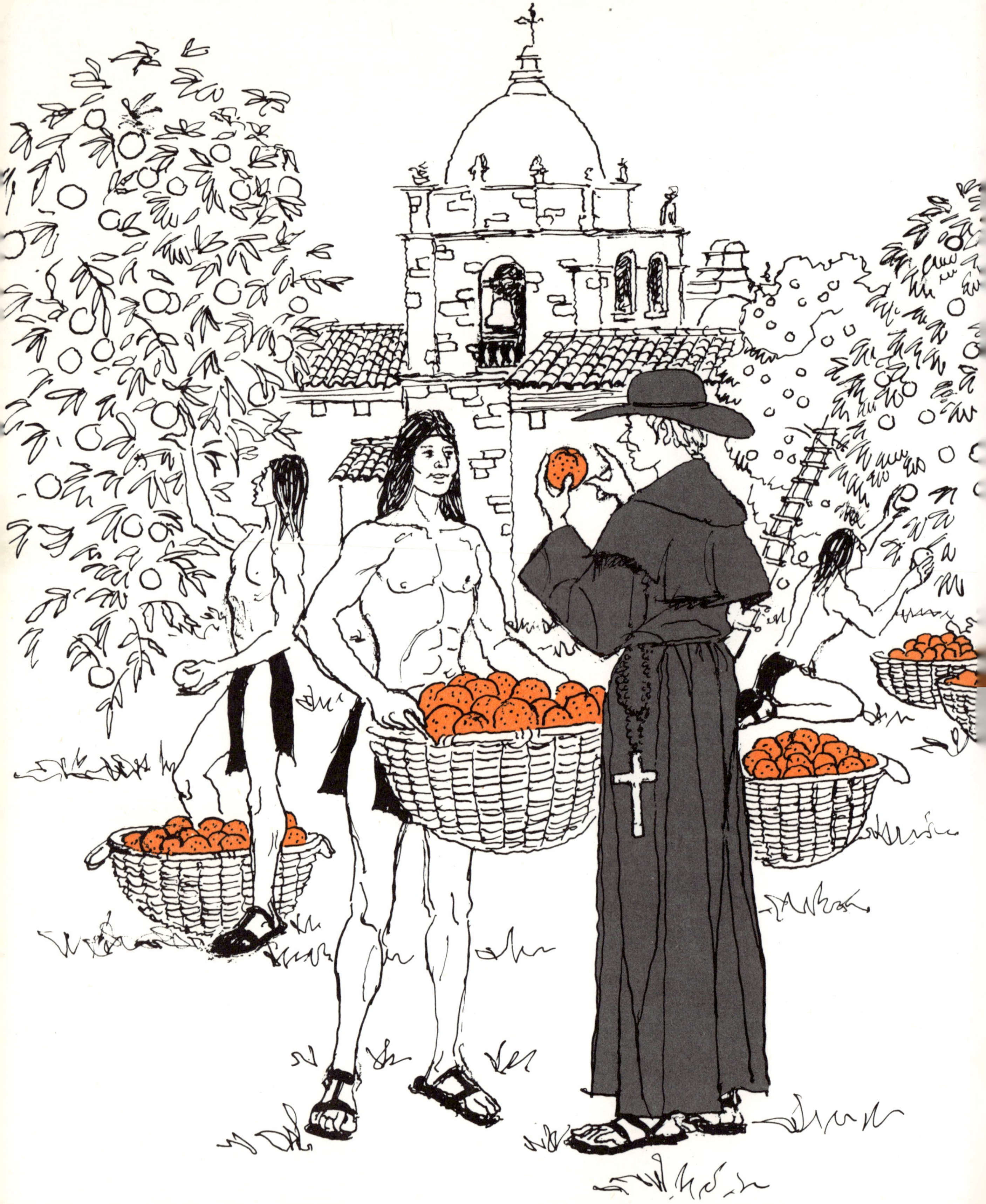

Sweet oranges probably first came from southeastern Asia, southern China, or India. People were eating them in southern Europe by the fifteenth century. About a hundred years later, Spaniards brought the orange with them when they explored the New World. They planted orange trees in what later became the state of Florida. In the last half of the eighteenth century, Spanish missionaries planted oranges in California. Today both states are important orange growers.

Oranges are grown in warm countries all over the world. They are the world's second leading fruit crop—apples are first. The United States is the largest orange grower in the world. Spain, Japan, Brazil, Italy,

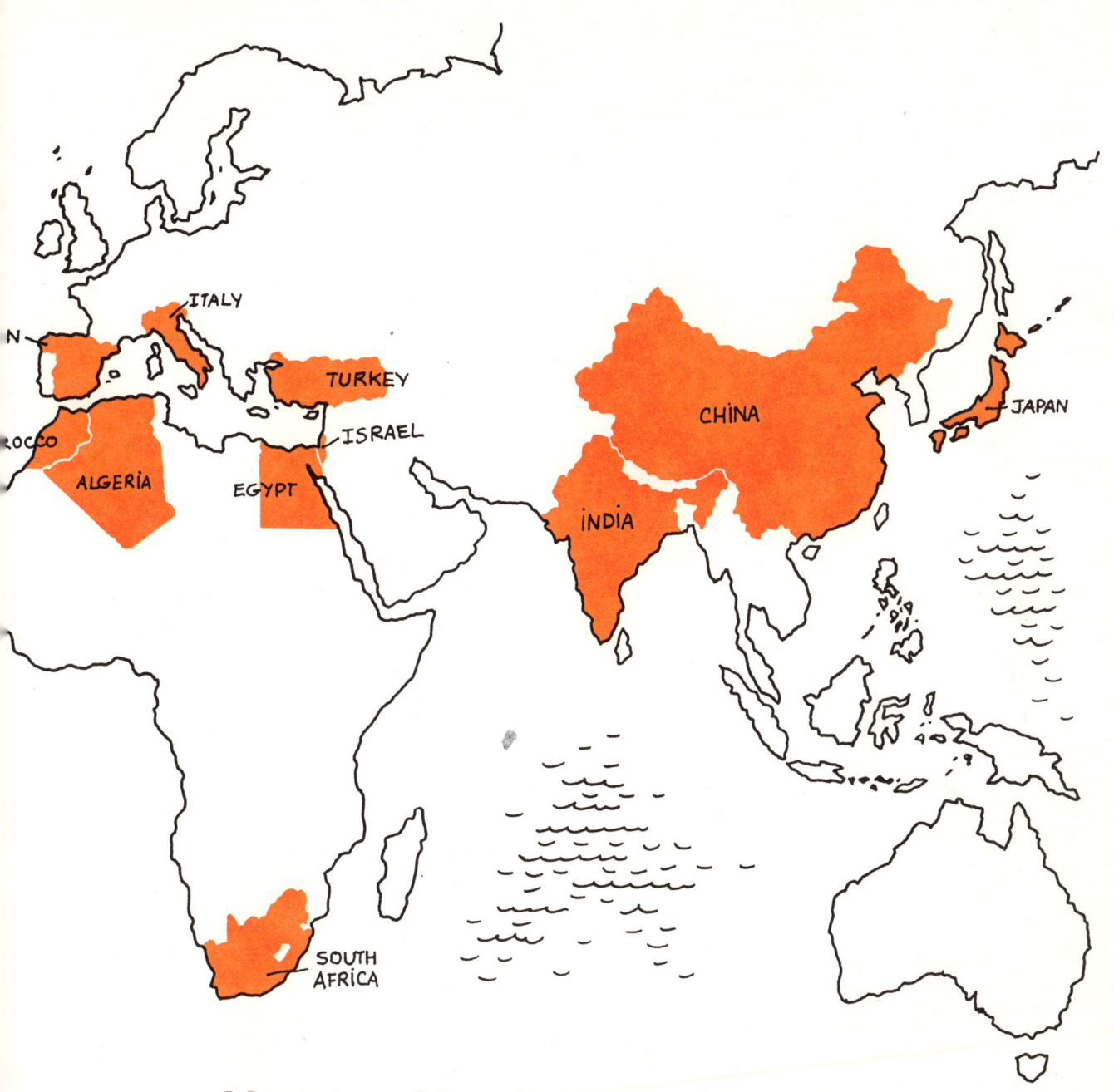

Mexico, and Israel are other important growers. But oranges are also grown in Argentina, Egypt, India, Morocco, Algeria, South Africa, Turkey, and China.

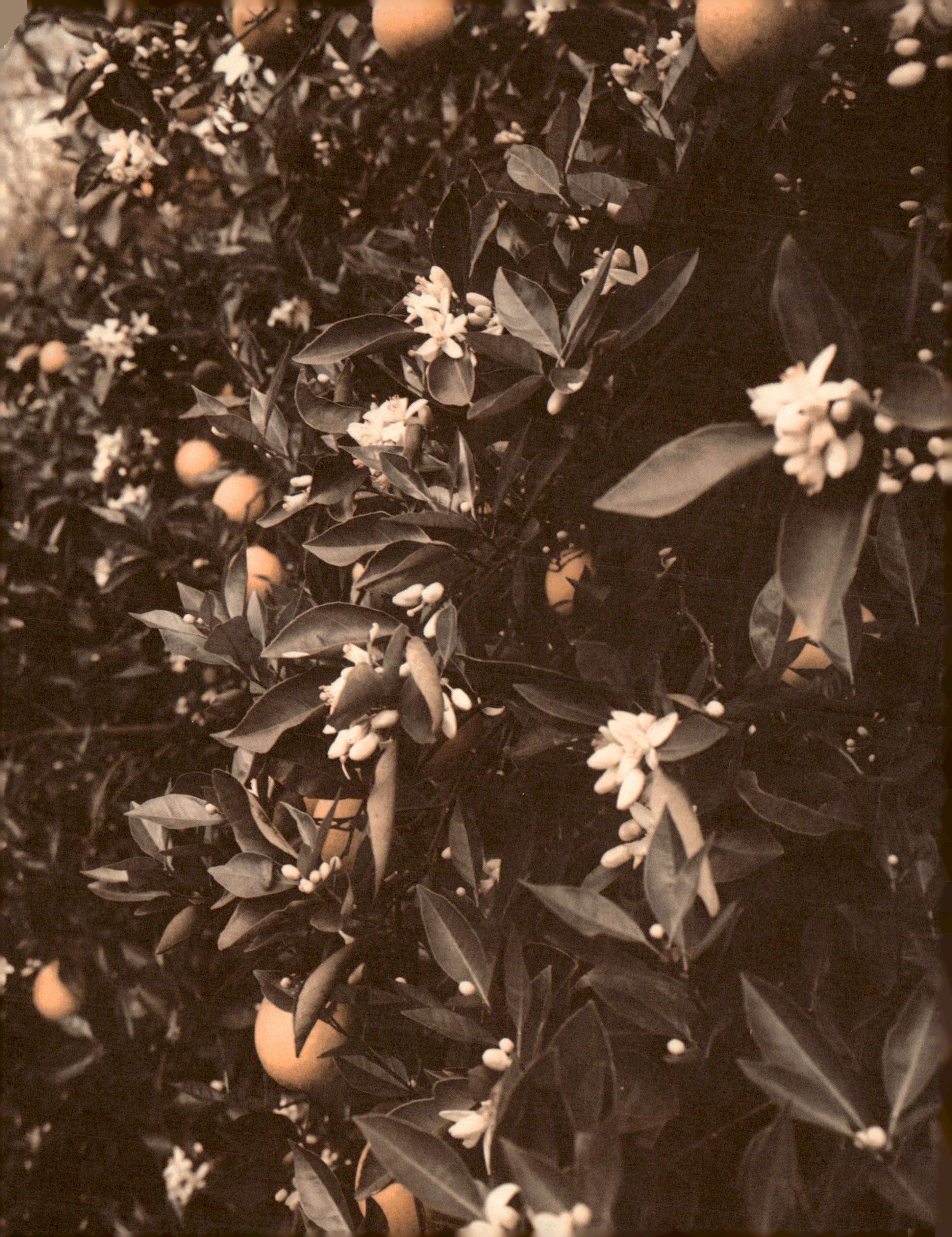

Florida Citrus Commission

Oranges grow on medium-sized evergreen trees. A group of orange trees is called a grove. The beautiful orange tree has a rounded top and pointed leaves. When in bloom, its pretty white flowers have a lovely smell. That is why orange blossoms are often used as a decoration at weddings or other special occasions. The tree usually blooms in spring, but it can also bloom in midsummer.

U. S. D. A. Photograph

The fruit of the orange tree is the orange itself. It is round or sort of oval-shaped. Its color may range from pale to very bright orange. The peel is easily removed from the pulp, which is the part you eat. Depending on the kind of orange, it may take from eight to fifteen months to ripen.

Oranges are a very good food. They are rich in vitamins A,B, and C. The juice has sugars, citric acid, and mineral salts which are good to eat.

There are three main kinds of cultivated oranges.

The popular *sweet orange* is the kind most grown in the United States. The tree is about 20 feet (6.096 meters) high but may grow to 35 feet (10.668 meters.) It bears round fruit and very fragrant flowers. It has names such as Washington Navel, Valencia, and Hamlin.

Sour, or *Seville, oranges* are used in making marmalade. The roots of the strong sour orange tree are used to graft other kinds of orange trees. The tree rarely grows higher than 25 feet (7.62 meters). Its fruit is a very bright color.

Mandarin oranges are not oranges! They are a citrus fruit. Mandarins look like small, flat oranges. They are known for their good taste. The trees are smaller than sweet or sour orange trees. Some kinds of mandarins are Temple oranges, tangerines, and tangelos. The tangelo is a cross between a tangerine and a grapefruit.

Growing oranges is a big business. Therefore, growers spend a lot of time making sure their trees bear fruit.

1.

2.

3.

4.

Five steps in budding.

All photographs—Florida Department of Citrus

5.

Young orange trees are usually grown from seeds in a nursery for one to two years. Then they are "budded." This means that a small part of a young orange tree is grafted on, or joined to, the seedling. A budded tree will produce fruit in three to five years. A tree grown from a seed takes 10 to 12 years to bear fruit!

A budded tree does not grow quite as tall as a seed tree. So it is easier to pick the fruit from a budded tree. Budding allows the grower to breed certain things into a tree, such as making it stronger to fight diseases. After budding, the young trees are put back in the nursery for a year. Then they are set out in the orange groves.

Florida Department of Citrus

An orange grove.

Orange trees may be "pruned," which means that branches may be cut away. Pruning can control the size and shape of the tree. It can also let more sunshine reach the inner parts of the tree.

Orange trees are not very fussy about the soil in which they grow—as long as they get enough water and minerals. But orange trees *are* very fussy about the temperature in which they grow. They must have warm weather. Orange trees cannot take more than a light frost without damage to the fruit. Sometimes orange growers wrap the

Smudge pots.

Florida Department of Citrus

trees in heavy material to protect them from the cold. Growers in California and other places use smudge pots. These are containers that burn oil or some other fuel to warm the air around the trees and keep the frost away.

Because temperature is so important to orange trees, it is not surprising that Florida and California are the leading "orange states." Texas and Arizona are important orange growers, too.

The first Florida orange groves were planted in the northern part of the state. Then came the winter of 1894-95. A temperature of 14° F. (-10° C.) killed almost the entire orange crop. After that, groves were planted in warmer central and southern Florida. The harvest season is from mid-October to late June. Most Florida oranges are used to make fresh or frozen orange juice.

RECIPES USING ORANGES

REFRESHING ORANGE PUNCH

1 quart of orange juice
4 slices of apple
1 banana, sliced
5 maraschino cherries
ice cubes

Prepare this punch just before you are ready to serve it. Mix the orange juice and fruit in a large pitcher. Add ice cubes and stir until well chilled. Pour.

NO-BAKING ORANGE BALLS

1 package (7¼ ounces) vanilla wafers, crushed
¾ cup grated coconut
½ cup frozen concentrated orange juice, undiluted
Confectioner's sugar

In a bowl, combine wafer crumbs, coconut, and concentrated orange juice. Mix well. Form into balls, about one inch in diameter. Roll the balls in a little confectioner's sugar. Store overnight in refrigerator in a covered container. Makes about three dozen.

FROZEN ORANGE POPSICLES

1 6-ounce can of frozen concentrated orange juice
1½ cans of water (use orange juice can)
15 1-ounce paper cups
15 wooden spoons or sticks

Mix orange juice and water. Pour evenly into the paper cups. Put cups into freezer. When the juice is slightly frozen, place a wooden stick or spoon into each cup. Then, freeze until solid. To remove a popsicle from the cup, push up on the bottom until the popsicle slides out.

If you can't find paper cups, just pour the juice into freezer trays and use ice cube dividers to separate the popsicles.

California's first large grove was at the San Gabriel Mission in 1804. Today the state's major orange-growing areas are in the south and north-central parts, and in the deserts. California has a longer growing season than Florida.

Valencia oranges are harvested from about May 1 to November 1. If you eat an orange during the summer months, you can be pretty sure it is a Valencia. Navel oranges are picked from about November 1 to May 1. The navel orange gets its strange name because of a small "bump" that sticks out from the peel. It looks a little like a human navel, or "belly button."

A Valencia orange in early stage of development.

U.S.D.A. Photograph

Orange pickers on the island of Cyprus.

United Nations Photograph

Orange trees in Florida and California can bear fruit for 50 years! But in Texas, trees last only about 20 years. One reason may be that there is more salt in Texas soil. A "champion" orange tree in southern California, near Pasadena, bore fruit for 67 years. It grew to 33 feet (10.058 meters) high, and its trunk, measured one foot above the ground, was five feet, seven inches (170.18 centimeters) around!

Even though orange trees can live a long time in good soil and a warm climate, they do have enemies. Grasshoppers, fruit flies, and aphids attack oranges. Sprays and dustings are used to keep these pests away. Virus and fungus are enemies, too. Foot rot can kill the bark, which will kill the tree. One way growers fight these diseases is to breed young plants that are strong enough to fight off a virus or fungus.

When oranges are ripe, they are picked by hand. Pickers use ladders to reach the fruit if it is too high. If the oranges will be sold as fresh fruit, they are cut from the tree with small clippers. The orange grower doesn't want the fruit to be damaged. If they are to be sold as frozen or canned, they are just pulled from the tree.

After harvesting, the oranges leave the grove for the cannery or packing plant. At the cannery, the fruit is washed and squeezed, and the juice is processed. Or the fruit is cleaned and peeled and canned.

At the packing plant, fresh oranges go through many steps before they are ready for market. First, they are washed in hot soapy water. Next, they are scrubbed by revolving brushes. They are rinsed three times before they are dried by air blowing over a moving belt. Then they are sorted according to size and waxed. Finally, they are packed in bags or cartons to be shipped to market.

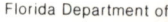

The fresh fruit also may be dyed with orange color before it is shipped to market. The dyed color makes the orange look more appetizing. Oranges from California usually don't have to be dyed because their color develops naturally.

Oranges are used for more than just food. In Spain, the flower, young fruit, and twigs go into the making of oil. In France, the blossoms go into perfume. Orange seeds make salad oil, and orange juice is used in syrups. And, of course, orange blossoms make beautiful decorations all over the world.

But you probably like oranges best in their usual form—as cold, tasty juice in the morning, or a fresh, plump fruit in your lunchbox.

GLOSSARY

Breeding:	to reproduce, and usually improve, the quality of plants or animals by controlling their growth pattern.
Budded:	when part of a plant is attached to a second plant to help it produce flowers or fruit.
Cannery:	a factory that processes food and puts it into cans.
Citric acid:	a pleasant-tasting substance found in citrus plants and often used for flavoring.
Citrus:	the family of trees or shrubs grown in warm climates for their fruit.
Clippers:	a tool used for cutting.
Cultivate:	grow a crop.
Evergreen:	a plant that does not lose its leaves in fall, but stays green all year round.
Fruit:	the edible product of a seed plant.
Fungus:	a parasite plant that causes disease.
Genus:	a class, group, or kind of biological species identified by common characteristics or features.
Graft:	to join two parts together to grow as one.
Grove:	a group of fruit or nut trees planted together.
New World:	the Western Hemisphere; North, South, and Central America.
Nursery:	a place where young plants are started and grown.
Peel:	the skin on a fruit.
Process:	to prepare a product for market in a factory.
Pulp:	the soft, edible part of a fruit.
Seedling:	a young plant grown from a seed.
Virus:	a small living organism that causes disease.
Vitamins:	any of several substances that are necessary to the health of most animals and plants.

INDEX

Algeria, 7
aphids, 25
Argentina, 7
Arizona, 20
Asia, southeastern, 5
balls, orange, 21
Brazil, 6
breeding, 14, 16
budded trees, 14, 15, 16
California, 5, 19, 20, 22, 24, 29
cannery, 27
China, southern, 5, 7
citric acid, 11
citrus fruits, 3, 12
decoration, 9, 29
disease, 16, 25
dyed oranges, 29
Egypt, 7
enemies, orange trees, 25
evergreen trees, 9
Florida, 5, 20, 22, 24
flower, orange, 9, 29
foot rot, 25
fruit-bearing years, 24
fruit, citrus, 3, 12
fruit flies, 25
fruit, orange, 10
frost damage, 18, 19
fungus, 25
genus, 3
grafting, 15
grapefruit, 3, 13
grasshoppers, 25
grove, 9, 16
growing time, 10, 15, 16, 24
Hamlin, 11
harvesting, 20, 22, 26
India, 5, 7
Israel, 6
Italy, 6
Japan, 6
lemons, 3
limes, 3
Mandarin oranges, 12

marmalade, 12
Mexico, 6
mineral salts, 11
missionaries, 5
Morocco, 7
navel orange, 22
New World, 5
nursery, 15, 16
oil, 29
orange blossoms, 9, 29
orange juice, 20, 27, 29
orange pops, 21
packing plant, 27, 28
perfume, 29
protection (frost), 19
pruning, 18
pulp, 10
punch, orange, 21
recipes, 21
salad oil, 29
San Gabriel Mission, 22
seedlings, 15
seed trees, 16
Seville oranges, 12
smudge pots, 19
sour oranges, 12
South Africa, 7
Spain, 6
Spaniards, 5
sugar, 11
sweet orange, 3, 5, 11
syrups, 29
tangelos, 13
tangerines, 13
temperature, 18
Temple oranges, 13
Texas, 20, 24
Turkey, 7
United States, 6
Valencia, 11, 22
virus, 25
vitamins, 11
Washington Navel, 11

About the Author:

Franklin Watts was born in Sioux City, Iowa. He lived in the Middle West for a considerable part of his lifetime, so the subject of raising as well as eating good food comes naturally.

Mr. Watts was the founder of two publishing houses under his own name — one in the United States and one in London. As a publisher Franklin Watts specializes in books for the young and his previous titles have also been directed to young audiences. "Children are very curious creatures and it is my aim and purpose in what I write to satisfy some of their curiosity," Mr. Watts says. "In fact, I hope to increase their desire for more information. While there have been books on food for the young, most of them have started with growing or the geography of foods. Here I am starting right where the child is — the fun of eating the food — so these books are planned working back from the food in the dish to the place where it is grown."

About the Artist:

Robert Ulm, a Chicago resident, has been an advertising and editorial artist in both New York and Chicago. Mr. Ulm is a successful painter as well as an illustrator. In his spare time he enjoys fishing and playing tennis.